THE RHODE ISLAND COAST

A PHOTOGRAPHIC PORTRAIT

Photography by Jim McElholm

Other Titles by
PILOTPRESS & TWIN LIGHTS PUBLISHERS

Cape Ann: A Photographic Portrait

Kittery to the Kennebunks: A Photographic Portrait

*The Mystic Coast–Stonington to New London:
A Photographic Portrait*

Boston's South Shore: A Photographic Portrait

The White Mountains: A Photographic Portrait

Upper Cape Cod: A Photographic Portrait

First published in the United States of America by
PilotPress Publishers, Inc.
110 Westchester Road
Newton, Massachusetts 02458
Telephone: (617) 332-0703
www.PilotPress.com
and
Twin Light Publishers, Inc.
Ten Hale Street
Rockport, Massachusetts 01966
Telephone: (978) 546-7398

ISBN 0-9677537-1-6

10 9 8 7 6 5 4 3 2 1

Designer: Leeann Leftwich
          Email: clldesign@aol.com

Printed in China

THE RHODE ISLAND COAST

A PHOTOGRAPHIC PORTRAIT

Photography by Jim McElholm

PILOTPRESS PUBLISHERS • TWIN LIGHTS PUBLISHERS

RHODE ISLAND

BRISTOL

W. GREENWICH

N. KINGSTOWN

PORTSMOUTH

WICKFORD

RICHMOND

MIDDLETOWN

KINGSTON

NEWPORT

CHARLESTOWN

POINT JUDITH

WESTERLEY

WATCH HILL

ATLANTIC OCEAN

BLOCK ISLAND

INTRODUCTION

Rhode Island is known as the "Ocean State", which is appropriate when you consider that it measures forty eight miles long and thirty seven miles wide but, has a coastline of four hundred miles including thirty six islands. Divided almost in half by Narragansett Bay, all corners of the state are within a short drive from the coast.

The independent character of Rhode Island has been developing since religious groups from Massachusetts, fleeing persecution, founded it in 1636. Rhode Island became a haven for political and religious refugees. The ports of Providence and Newport were engaged in trade and shipbuilding as well as the less than legal occupations of privateering and later, slavery.

England and Rhode Island fought regularly over trade, which resulted in the colony declaring itself independent on May 4, 1776, two months prior to the issuance of the Declaration of Independence. Rhode Island reluctantly ratified the Constitution in 1790, the last of the thirteen original states to do so, and then only after threats of tariff barriers and invasion were issued.

The independent streak continued into the 1920's when Rhode Island was one of two states to reject the Volstead Act. Once Prohibition was a fact, Rhode Islanders took full advantage of the coast's many hidden coves and inlets to become rumrunners.

Along with the independence of its inhabitants, Rhode Island had natural resources in several swift-running rivers that provided power for manufacturing operations. Textiles and jewelry became an important part of the economy and remains so to this day.

Presently Rhode Island provides the visitor with diversity in a small space; from the urban life of Providence, to the sophistication of Newport, and the rolling pasturelands of South County. The geography of Rhode Island is varied with rugged hillsides in the north, barrier beaches along the southern coast, steep headlands in the east, and quiet pastures and woods in the southeast. Narragansett Bay provides the state with two popular forms of recreation; swimming and boating.

TABLE OF CONTENTS

Newport is situated on the southwest coast of Aquidneck Island at the mouth of Narragansett Bay. An active waterfront combined with majestic mansions, a variety of museums, shops, art galleries, and festivals lure multinational visitors by the thousands. The temperate summer climate which years ago attracted wealthy New Yorkers, who built their fabulous "summer cottages," now attracts mariners from all corners of the world to this beautiful harbor.

NEWPORT

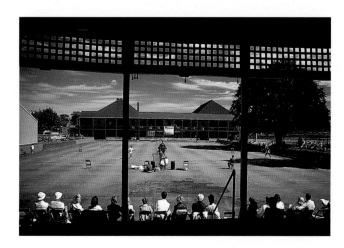

The International Tennis Hall of
Fame in the Newport Casino is
a Mecca for tennis buffs and all
who enjoy the history of the
game and the many famous
players. The grass courts in the
center of the buildings host the
annual National Grass Court
championships.

NEWPORT ART MUSEUM

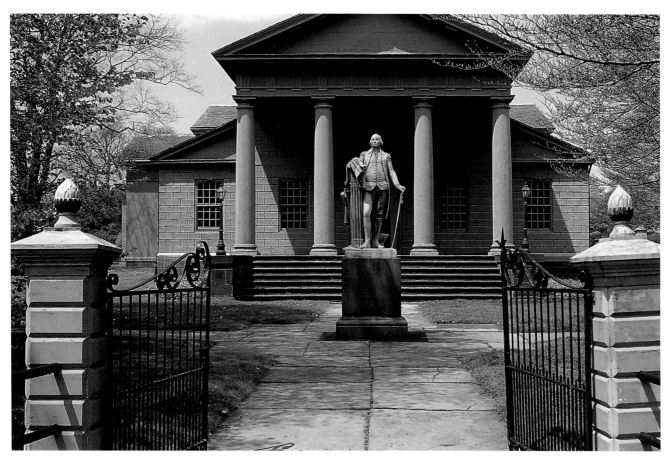

The Redwood Library and
Athenaeum built in the
Palladian style, is the oldest
library building in continuous
service. The building, designed
by Peter Harrison has been
enlarged four times. Built of
wood, as are most of the buildings in Newport, the siding has
been blasted to look like stone.
At the front entrance to the
library is a statue of George
Washington.

OPPOSITE

The Newport Art Museum,
designed by Richard Morris
Hunt, displays changing
exhibitions of contemporary
and historical art.

The Newport County court-
house is a beautiful Federal
building in the heart of
Newport.

The Old Stone Mill has been
attributed to Vikings, Native-
Americans and English colonists
depending on the storyteller.
There is no real evidence to
indicate why it was built, who
built it or when it was built;
however, it stands in a lovely
park and is well worth a visit.

The Newport Jazz Festival is a very popular part of Newport's cultural offerings held on the grounds of historic Fort Adams overlooking the harbor. The Festival is an annual event featuring the legends of jazz as well as up-and-coming musicians.

Sailboats abound in the harbor, carrying on Newport's long-standing tradition as a seaport.

This busy harbor is host to different crafts of all shapes and sizes, many of which are available to the public for tours around the harbor.

Windsurfing in the harbor is not for the faint-hearted!

Cruise ships anchor off Fort
Adams commanding a full
view of Newport Harbor and
sending their passengers into
port on tenders.

The Newport Bridge spans
Narragansett Bay from
Newport to Jamestown
providing a lovely backdrop
for mariners approaching
Newport Harbor.

Tall ships sail majestically
into the harbor at Newport.

Polo made its American
debut in Newport County.
Present day players and
devotees are equally enthu-
siastic about this sport.

Authentically dressed militia units line up for the St. Patrick's Day parade.

Fife and drum corps units are always popular with spectators.

ABOVE

Elegant wrought iron gates guard Marble House.

OPPOSITE

Marble House, one of Newport's jewels, is a spectacular "summer cottage" built for William K. Vanderbilt, designed by Richard Hunt and modeled after the Petit Trianon at Versailles.

Belcourt Castle, designed by
Richard Hunt for Oliver Hazard
Perry Belmont, is an elegant
background for a sumptuous
23-carat golden coach.

The Chinese Tea House was
constructed without facilities
for making tea so a tiny
railroad was constructed to
transport the tea and the
servers to the teahouse.
It is a beautiful spot to visit
at Marble House.

Rolling lawns and beautiful flower gardens are a must see for visitors at Rosecliff.

Rosecliff, designed in 1900 by Stanford White for Hermann Oelrichese, boasted the largest ball-room of all the mansions in Newport.

An aerial view of The Breakers, one-time summer home of Cornelius Vanderbilt, was designed by Richard Hunt and was the largest most opulent of the Newport mansions.

ABOVE

Hammersmith Farm, the
former home of Jacqueline
Bouvier Kennedy and
sometimes summer White
House, is now a museum with
formal gardens and playhouse.

OPPOSITE

Tower building overlooking
the ocean at Hammersmith
Farm is a guesthouse and is
still owned by the Hugh D.
Auchincloss family.

TOP

The Elms, the magnificent estate of the late E. J. Berwind (a Philadelphia coal magnate), is best noted for the 14 acres of grounds with sunken French gardens, exotic trees, shrubs, and teahouses.

ABOVE

Grandeur overlooking the ocean.

OPPOSITE

An aerial view looking back at some of the mansions from the ocean side.

ABOVE
Castle Hill lighthouse at sunset.

OPPOSITE
Newport Bridge silhouetted
against a beautiful sunset.

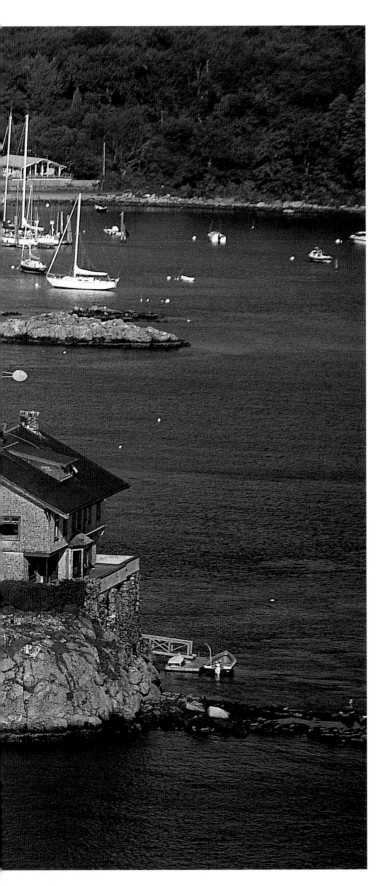

ABOVE

An anchor lends atmosphere to picturesque Bowen's wharf.

OPPOSITE

A most interesting residence at the entrance to Newport Harbor.

ABOVE

Fort Adams, designed to be the most heavily armed fort in America, guards the entrance to Newport Harbor.

OPPOSITE

A beautiful day in Newport harbor photographed over Bannister wharf.

FOLLOWING PAGE

From the air it is easy to see why Newport is a sailor's haven.

Richard Munday designed Trinity Church after designs by Christopher Wren. The church is notable for its graceful spire, Tiffany stained glass windows and its triple-deck wineglass pulpit.

Newport's Colonial homes are beautifully decorated to welcome visitors for the holiday season.

FOLLOWING PAGE
Christmas on the wharf.

ABOVE

Newport is noted for the lovely architecture of its gracious homes. By the time the Revolution was over and at the end of a three-year occupation by the British and the Hessians, Newport was a depleted city monetarily and no longer a major port. Newport residents, for the most part, were too poor to rebuild their colonial style homes and thus the homes were preserved.

RIGHT AND OPPOSITE

Charming houses line the streets of Newport while Winter adds its own decorations to the Colonial architecture.

ABOVE

The variety of the styles of architecture adds to the charm of Newport.

OPPOSITE

Colonial red graces this Newport house.

An aerial view of the old
windmill on the grounds of
Prescott Farm, Middletown.
Prescott Farm was the home of
Mrs. John Overing whose guest,
British general William Prescott,
was taken prisoner by Col.
William Barton and a band of
raiding colonists.

PORTSMOUTH,

MIDDLETOWN,

& BRISTOL

ABOVE

Beavertail lighthouse at the
southern tip of Conanicut
Island is the third lighthouse
established in America (1749)
and can be reached by crossing
the Newport Bridge from
Newport to Jamestown.

OPPOSITE

The working windmill on
Prescott Farm, Middletown.

Animals parade through the gardens in Portsmouth, the first town in America to be founded by a woman, Anne Hutchinson.

Menagerie of animals at the Green Animals Topiary Gardens in Portsmouth.

Blithewold is a elegant 45-room mansion in Bristol built by Augustus Van Wickle for his wife The original mansion burned to the ground in 1907. Mrs. Van Wickle built the present house the following year. The gardens were laid out by New York architect John De Wolf with 33 acres of landscaped grounds famous for beautiful Japanese gardens and approximately 50,000 flowering spring bulbs.

OPPOSITE

Everywhere the visitor turns there are more lovely gardens to enjoy.

The Japanese gardens at
Blithewold are a cool and
serene place to visit.

An airy gazebo, beautiful flow-
ers and comfortable chairs.
What more could a visitor
require.

Civil war monument in
historic Bristol, host of the
oldest 4th of July parade
in America.

The entrance to Wickford
harbor from the air.

WEST GREENWICH, WICKFORD
& NORTH KINGSTOWN

ABOVE

Native-American culture and dress is on display at this annual event.

LEFT

Visitors enjoy the colorful dress and dances displayed by this native-American.

OPPPOSITE

American Indian Federation Annual Powwow in West Greenwich.

89

ISSAC
REYNOLDS
1808

ABOVE

An artistic display shows off this garden shop's wares.

OPPOSITE

Approaching Wickford from the south by air shows off the waterside mansions.

ABOVE

An old-fashioned flower garden and picket fence surround this lovely shop.

OPPOSITE

Saunderstown, North Kingstown, home of artist Gilbert Stuart, the foremost Colonial portraitist best known for his portraits of George Washington. The Stuarts moved to Newport when young Gilbert was 10 years old.

FOLLOWING PAGE

A cluster of picturesque buildings surround the main house.

ABOVE AND LEFT
A quiet house and cottage beside a serene lily-filled pond.

OPPOSITE
Beautiful lilies at Smith Castle in North Kingstown, the only remaining example of the plantation houses that once covered this part of Rhode Island.

A tranquil country scene in Richmond.

RICHMOND & KINGSTON

ABOVE AND RIGHT

Richmond Country Club in Richmond:
A very scenic clubhouse and a quiet round
of golf shows another face of Rhode Island.

Waterfowl abound in tranquil ponds like this all over Rhode Island.

After the pond, Horseshoe Falls in Shannock, Richmond.

ABOVE

Green grass and lily ponds, a
rustic scene in Richmond is a
contrast to the seaside views
for which Rhode Island is
noted.

RIGHT

Water sports are plentiful in
South County as shown by
these canoeists.

OPPOSITE

Octagon House, Richmond is a
unique example of the varied
architecture to be found in
Rhode Island.

Hot Air Balloon Festival in Kingston
displays the variety of activities
available in South County.

ABOVE

Sitting in the shade on Roy Carpenter's beach in South Kingstown.

RIGHT

Sailboats at the dock in South Kingstown.

Point Judith, Jerusalem and
Galilee from the air.

POINT JUDITH, NARRAGANSETT,

JERUSALEM & GALILEE

ABOVE

The Towers is the last remaining section of the Narragansett Pier Casino destroyed by fire in 1900. This familiar landmark is a reminder of the rich heritage of the area.

OPPOSITE

Overlooking a beautiful salt marsh in Narragansett. A wide variety of wildlife and birds abound in these protected areas.

ABOVE

Roger E. Wheeler Memorial Beach in Narragansett is only one of the many lovely beaches along the southern coast of Rhode Island.

OPPOSITE

A quiet walk along Wheeler Beach.

BELOW

Flying a kite on Wheeler Beach is a family affair.

South County Museum at Canochet
Farms, a 174-acre park in
Narragansett.

A boat returning home to Narragansett. Boating is only one of the many sports in Rhode Island.

Point Judith lighthouse stands at the end of Harbor of Refuge, a safe haven for mariners.

ABOVE

Ferry returning to Galilee, a very active fishing
port, ferry depot and recreational boating center.

OPPOSITE

Point Judith lighthouse from the air. Point Judith is
also the site of a very active Coast Guard station.

Windsurfing in Ninigret
Pond, Charlestown.

CHARLESTOWN,
SOUTH COUNTY COAST, WESTERLY,
& WATCH HILL

ABOVE

East Matunuck State Beach another one of Rhode Island's "necklace" of beautiful beaches.

LEFT

Beach houses stand against the sky on Misquamicut Beach.

OPPOSITE

Braving the whims of the Atlantic Ocean, beach houses stand on Misquamicut Beach

A calm and quiet place to moor
a boat in Charlestown.

TOP LEFT

Sailing along the South County coast on a beautiful sunny day is a wonderful experience.

ABOVE LEFT

Clamming in South County. Clammers pull their baskets and pails (floating in inner tubes) behind them as they dig for the famous Rhode Island mollusks.

TOP RIGHT

A quiet pond in Charlestown reveals the variety of scenic spots in Rhode Island.

ABOVE RIGHT

A bird sanctuary in Charlestown.

West Fest Rodeo at Ninigret Park, Charlestown.

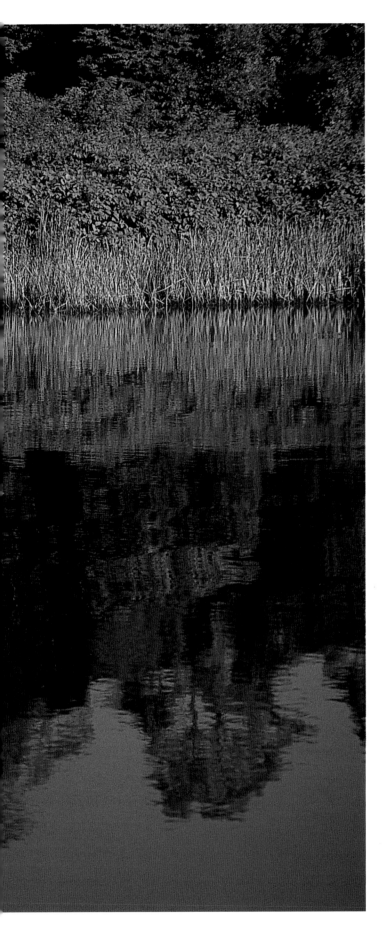

ABOVE

Sailboats anchored off Westerly. There are abundant harbors and mooring areas all along the coast in Rhode Island for the recreational boater.

OPPOSITE

Boathouse in Charlestown.

BELOW

Chillin' out in Westerly.

ABOVE LEFT
Home on the South County coast.

LEFT
The Ninigret Pond area in South County is another one of the beautiful wild areas behind the beaches along the coast.

BELOW LEFT
Westerly from the air.

House off the South County coast.

Watch Hill and Napatree are the southern-most points of Rhode Island. Napatree is noted for the long sandy beach and Watch Hill for its picturesque town and views overlooking the ocean.

Sunny afternoon from the
verandah of the Surf Inn,
Block Island

BLOCK ISLAND

Southeast Light on Mohegan Bluffs had to be moved back from the edge of the bluffs because of the extensive erosion over the years. This significant feat of engineering was carried out with a minimum of damage to the structure.

ABOVE

Overlooking Great Salt Pond from the rolling farmland. Block Island is one of the most unspoiled islands on the East coast.

LEFT

Aerial view of Old Harbor.

OPPOSITE

Southeast Light has one of the most powerful electric beacons on the East coast.

ABOVE

Great Salt Pond area features charming houses with beautiful views over the pond and surrounding land.

OPPOSITE

Sunset over Great Salt Pond, a very active and hospitable harbor.

BELOW

Arrival of the ferry at Old Harbor, which is noted for the many old-fashioned Victorian turreted and gingerbread-decorated hotels, shops and restaurants.

Southeast Light on Mohegan Bluffs is one of the most photographed lighthouses in the area.

Mohegan Bluffs rising 150 feet with wild roses in profusion on the top of the bluffs. There is a wooden staircase providing access to the foot of the bluffs.

Gingerbread decoration lends an old world air to the inn at Old Harbor and welcomes visitors from the mainland as they get off the ferry.

Sailing off Mohegan Bluffs is some of the best around and is just a short sail from the mainland.

Coast Guard station at the
entrance to Great Salt Pond.

ABOVE
Sailboat racing off Mohegan Bluffs.

OPPOSITE
Relaxation and recreation at the Sea Breeze Inn overlooking Spring House Pond.

Kayaking on one of the 365 ponds on Block Island.

One of Block Islands more unique examples of architecture.

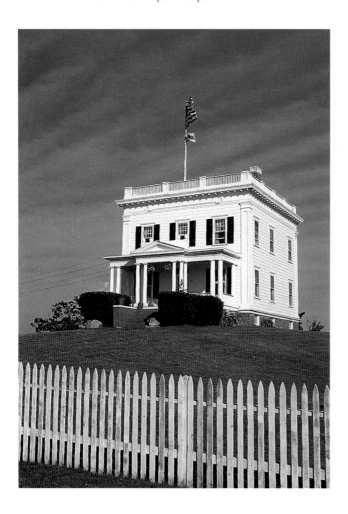

JIM McELHOLM

Jim McElholm began his career as a history teacher. In preparation for his classes, he traveled extensively, visiting the world's historical sights from the Pyramids of Egypt, Red Square in Moscow to the many wonders of Europe. He captured his excitement on film and used these images to supplement his classroom presentations.

This early introduction to photography inevitably paved the way for a full-time career as a professional travel photographer. Early in his photographic journey he became fascinated with scenic landscapes, history, and people immersed in their unique local culture. His assignments have taken him throughout North America, Europe, the Far East and the Caribbean.

Each experience provides a wonderful opportunity to capture the beauty of the people and landscapes on film. Jim's love of the "back roads" and his work with regional tourist bureaus have allowed him to document the hidden visual treasures found throughout New England. Visit his Internet site at www.SingleSourcePhoto.com to share his unique photographic discoveries. These photo-discovery tours will allow you to plan your visit to these beautiful areas. Don't forget to bring your camera. The ever-changing quality of light will provide you with a kaleidoscope of opportunities and colors that will stimulate your visual imagination.

BIBLIOGRAPHY

Rhode Island, An Explorer's Guide, Méras and Gannon, 2nd Edition, The Countryman Press, 1998.

Rhode Island, Rhode Island Tourism Division

The Architectural Heritage of Newport Rhode Island, Antoinette F. Downing and Vincent J. Scully, Jr., 2nd Edition, Bramhall House, 1967